S0-DUU-299

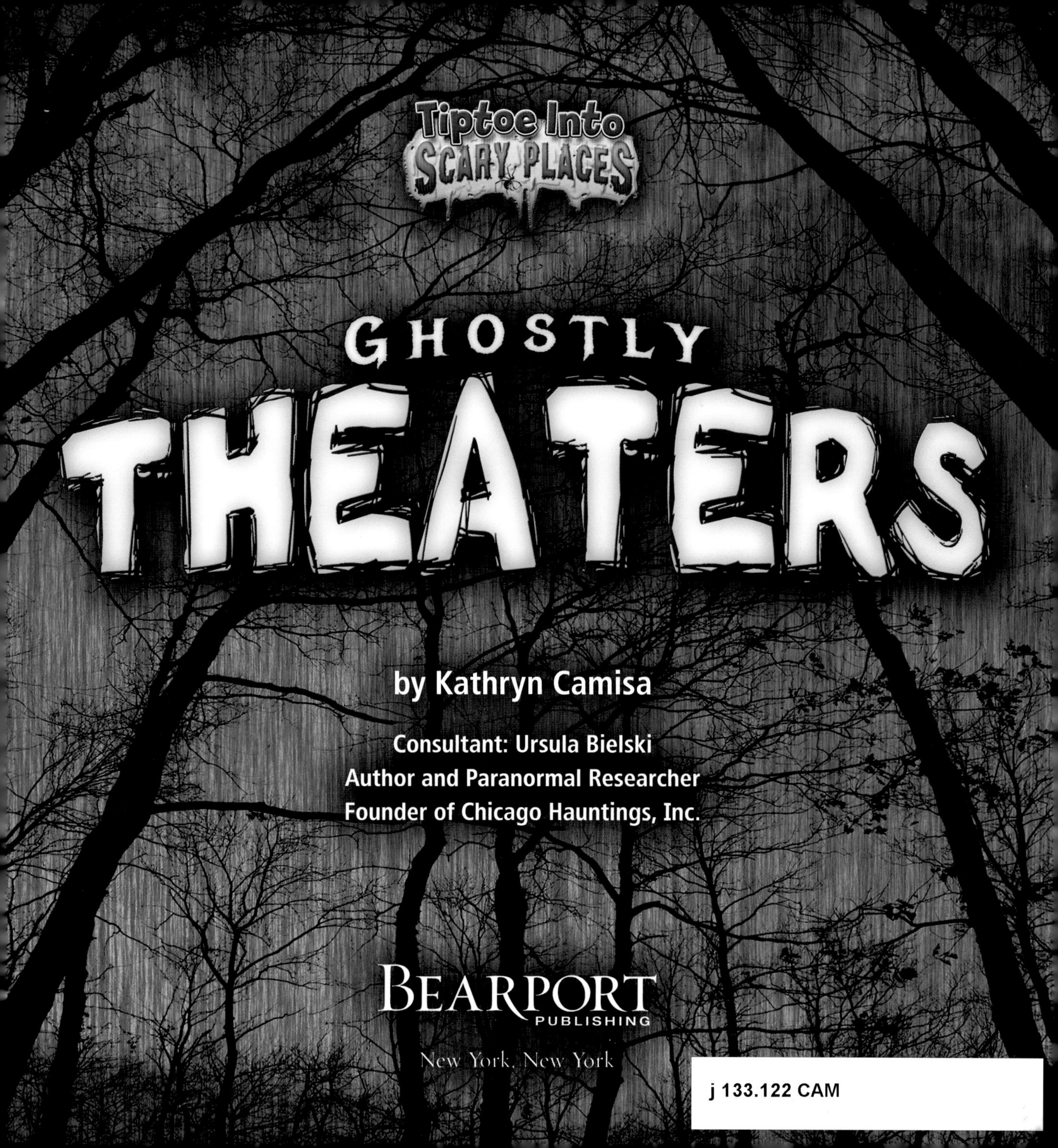

Tiptoe Into Scary Places

GHOSTLY THEATERS

by Kathryn Camisa

Consultant: Ursula Bielski
Author and Paranormal Researcher
Founder of Chicago Hauntings, Inc.

BEARPORT PUBLISHING

New York, New York

Credits

Cover, © Serge/Fotolia, © dusk/Fotolia, and © Alexandr Zacliraka/Shutterstock; TOC, © Greg Randles/Shutterstock; 4, © Rocksweeper/Shutterstock, © bondvit/Shutterstock, © Africa Studio/Shutterstock, © ID1974/Shutterstock, © James Steidl/Shutterstock, and © Potapov Alexander/Shutterstock; 6T, © LEE SNIDER PHOTO IMAGES/Shutterstock; 6B, © Arbaes/Dreamstime; 7, © Valentin Agapov/Shutterstock and © Mayer George/Shutterstock; 8T, © PenelopeB/iStock; 8B, © Eric Martin/Figarophoto/Redux; 9, Public Domain; 10L, © Everett Historical/Shutterstock; 10R, © GL Archive/Alamy Stock Photo; 11, © Chronicle/Alamy Stock Photo; 12, © Kamira/Shutterstock; 13, © Sean Pavone/Shutterstock and © ESOlex/Shutterstock; 14, © Predrag Vranic; 14–15, © Kamenetskiy Konstantin/Shutterstock and © Fer Gregory/Shutterstock; 16L, © katalinks/Shutterstock; 16R, © ostill/Shutterstock; 17, © Sergey Petrov/Shutterstock; 18, © Anthony Weller/VIEW Pictures Ltd/Alamy Stock Photo; 19, © Ellen McKnight/Alamy Stock Photo; 20, © Helen Johnson; 21L, © BRad06/CC BY-SA 4.0; 21R, © gcpics/Shutterstock; 23, © Kozlik/Shutterstock; 24, © muratart/Shutterstock.

Publisher: Kenn Goin
Senior Editor: Joyce Tavolacci
Creative Director: Spencer Brinker
Photo Researcher: Thomas Persano
Cover: Kim Jones

Library of Congress Cataloging-in-Publication Data

Names: Camisa, Kathryn, author.
Title: Ghostly theaters / by Kathryn Camisa.
Description: New York : Bearport Publishing Company, Inc., 2018. | Series: Tiptoe into scary places | Includes bibliographical references and index.
Identifiers: LCCN 2017007499 (print) | LCCN 2017017205 (ebook) | ISBN 9781684023219 (ebook) | ISBN 9781684022670 (library)
Subjects: LCSH: Haunted theaters—Juvenile literature. | Ghosts—Juvenile literature.
Classification: LCC BF1477.5 (ebook) | LCC BF1477.5 .C36 2018 (print) | DDC 133.1/22—dc23
LC record available at https://lccn.loc.gov/2017007499

For more information, write to Bearport Publishing Company, Inc., 45 West 21st Street, Suite 3B, New York, New York 10010. Printed in the United States of America.

10 9 8 7 6 5 4 3 2 1

CONTENTS

Ghostly Theaters

You find yourself alone in a dark, empty theater. The curtain has fallen, and it's **eerily** quiet. Then, suddenly, you hear footsteps coming from the stage. When you peek behind the heavy red curtain, however, the stage is empty! Could someone else be **lurking** in the theater?

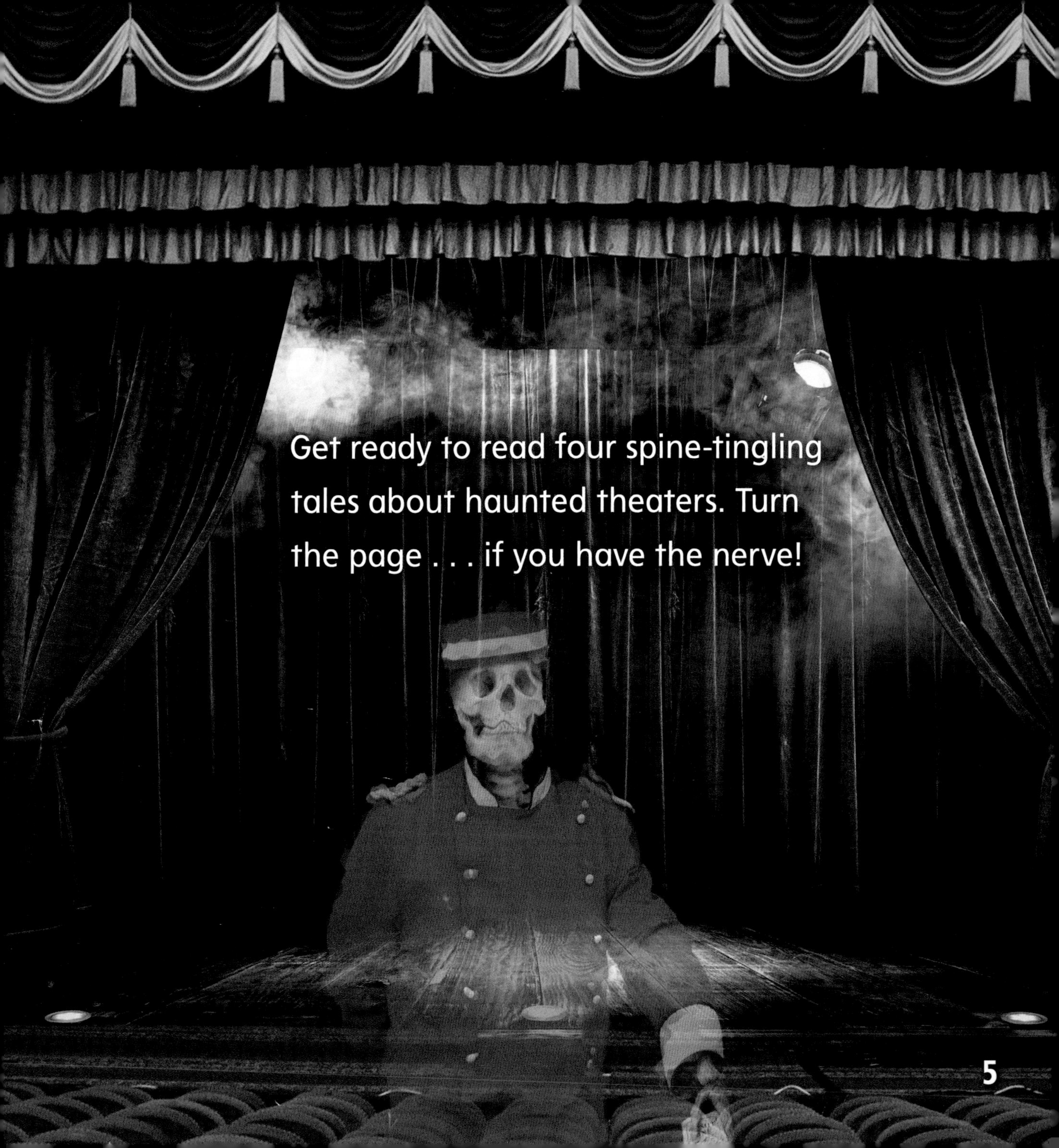

Get ready to read four spine-tingling tales about haunted theaters. Turn the page . . . if you have the nerve!

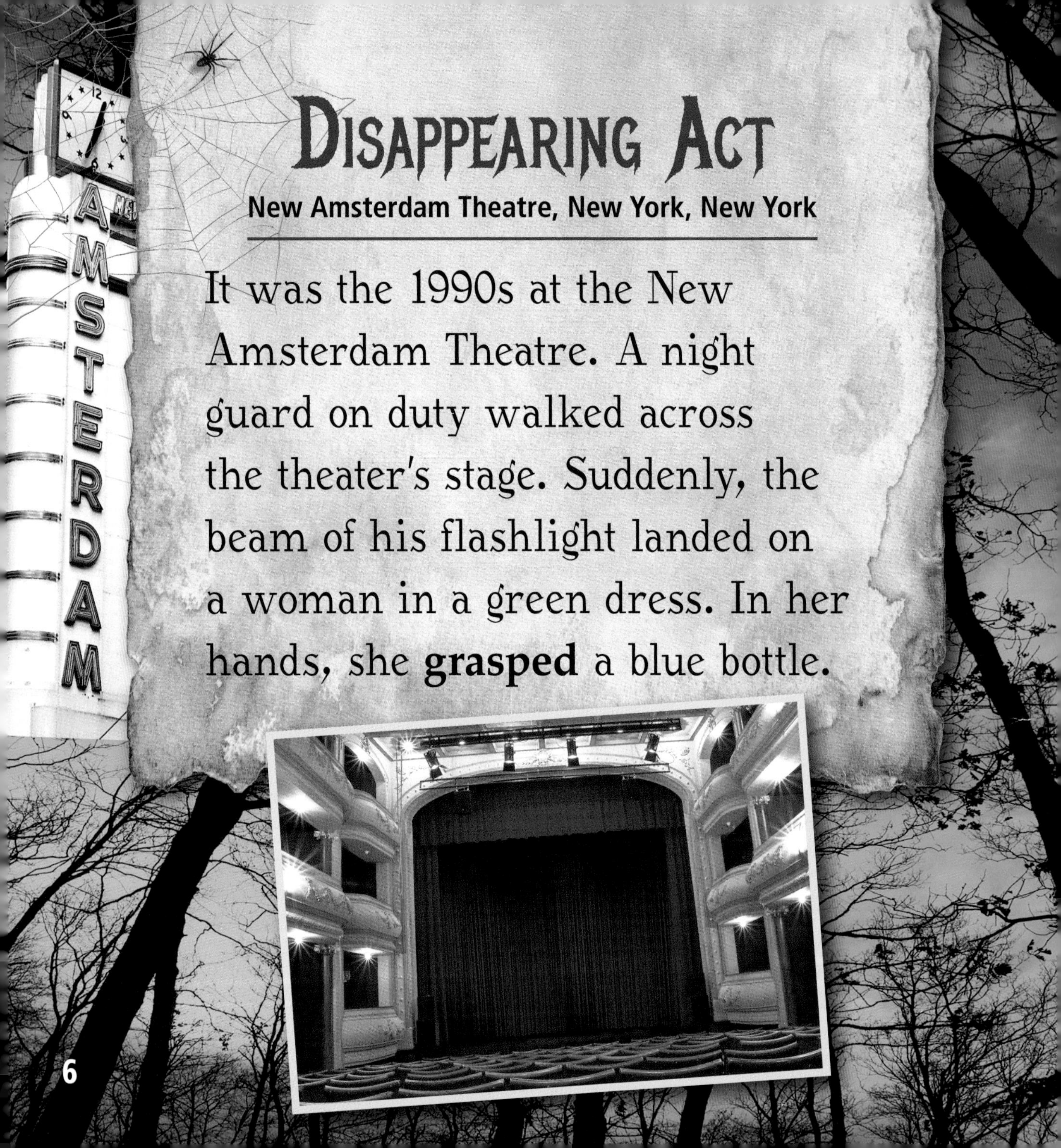

Disappearing Act

New Amsterdam Theatre, New York, New York

It was the 1990s at the New Amsterdam Theatre. A night guard on duty walked across the theater's stage. Suddenly, the beam of his flashlight landed on a woman in a green dress. In her hands, she **grasped** a blue bottle.

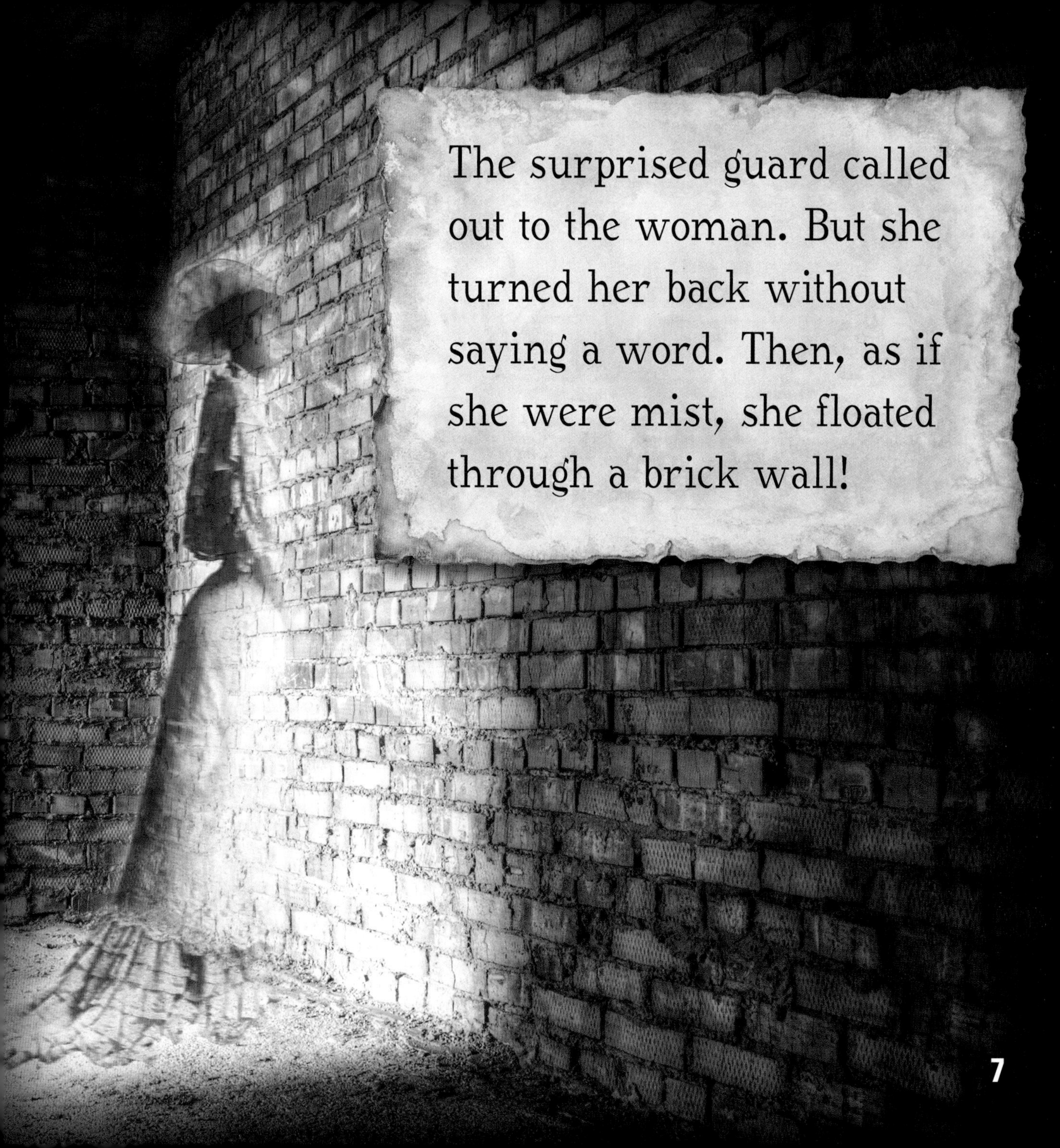

The surprised guard called out to the woman. But she turned her back without saying a word. Then, as if she were mist, she floated through a brick wall!

Many believe the guard had seen the **spirit** of Olive Thomas. Olive was a famous showgirl at the theater. Sadly, her life came to a **tragic** end.

On a cold December night in 1920, Olive lay awake. She reached for a blue bottle she thought contained sleeping pills. What she didn't realize was that it was filled with poison.

The hotel room where Olive Thomas died

Shortly after her death, people began to see Olive's ghost. It appeared on stage holding the same blue bottle.

Olive's ghost is so well known that people say "Good Night, Olive" when they leave the New Amsterdam Theatre.

A Bloody Crime

Ford's Theatre, Washington, DC

Ford's Theatre is one of the most famous theaters in America. However, it's known for more than its plays. A shocking murder happened there.

It was the night of April 14, 1865. President Abraham Lincoln and his wife, Mary, were watching a play.

President Abraham Lincoln

Bang! The booming sound of a gunshot rang out. Lincoln slumped over in his chair. Blood poured from his head. Hours later, the president was dead.

John Wilkes Booth was the man who shot Lincoln. He was angry because the South had lost the **Civil War**.

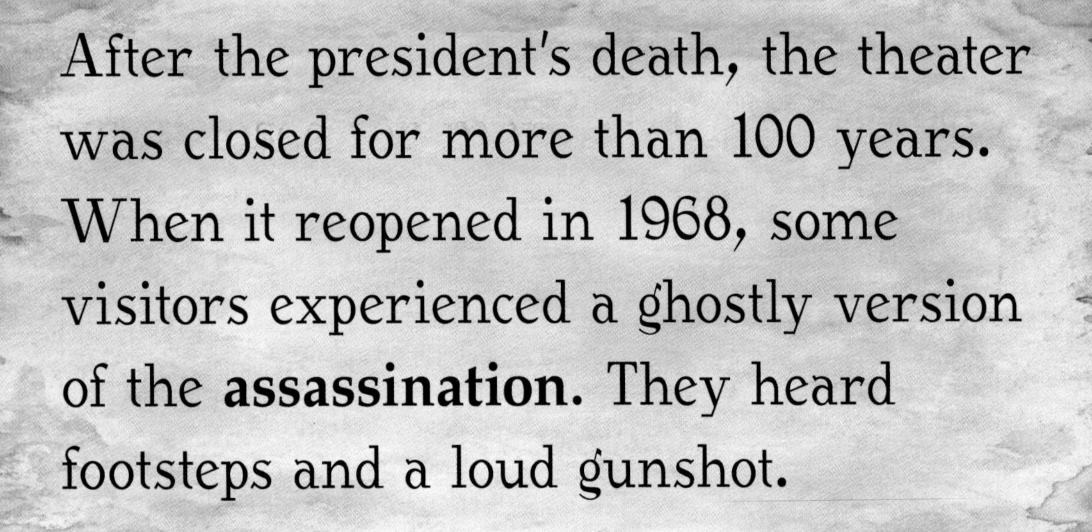

After the president's death, the theater was closed for more than 100 years. When it reopened in 1968, some visitors experienced a ghostly version of the **assassination.** They heard footsteps and a loud gunshot.

The gun used to kill President Lincoln

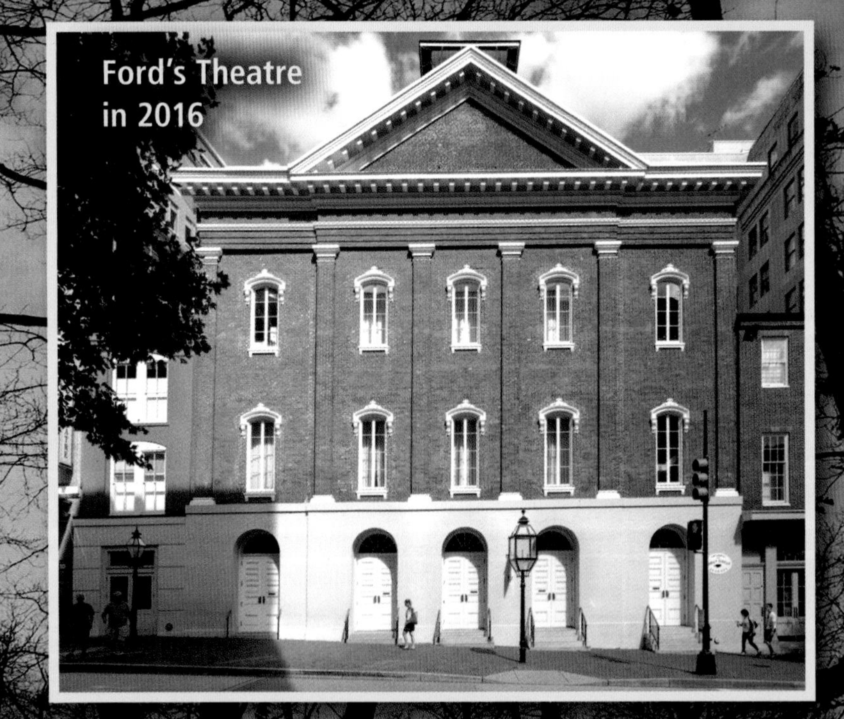

Ford's Theatre in 2016

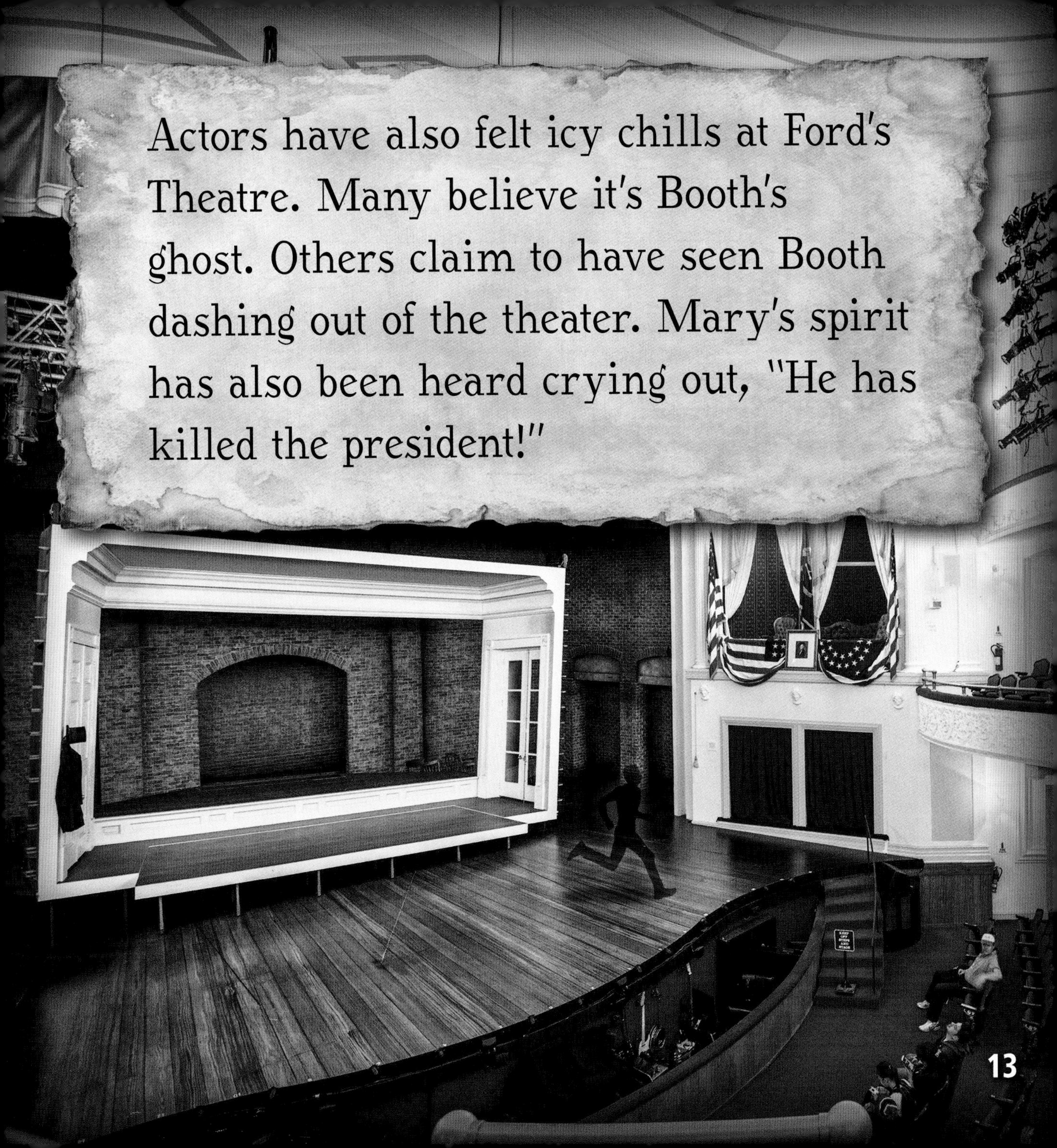

Actors have also felt icy chills at Ford's Theatre. Many believe it's Booth's ghost. Others claim to have seen Booth dashing out of the theater. Mary's spirit has also been heard crying out, "He has killed the president!"

Saved by a Spirit?

St. James Theatre, Wellington, New Zealand

It's almost showtime. Suddenly, the theater goes dark. A backstage worker searches for a light switch. Without knowing it, he comes very close to falling off the stage.

The St. James Theatre

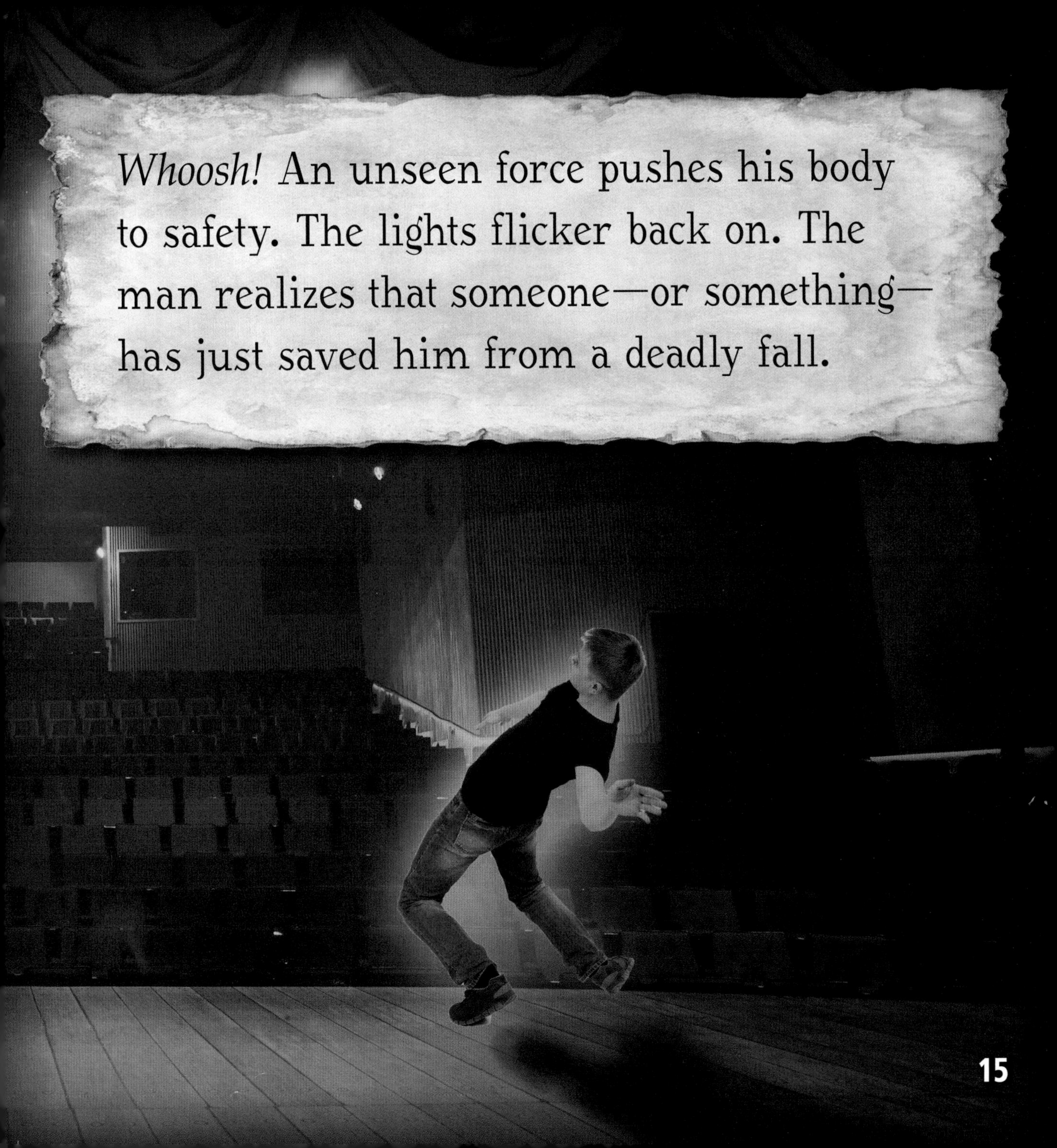

Whoosh! An unseen force pushes his body to safety. The lights flicker back on. The man realizes that someone—or something—has just saved him from a deadly fall.

So who saved the worker? Some believe it was the ghost of a Russian dancer. Many years before, the dancer had fallen to his death off the same stage. Ever since, a tall thin spirit has been seen in the theater. People have also heard footsteps when no one else is around.

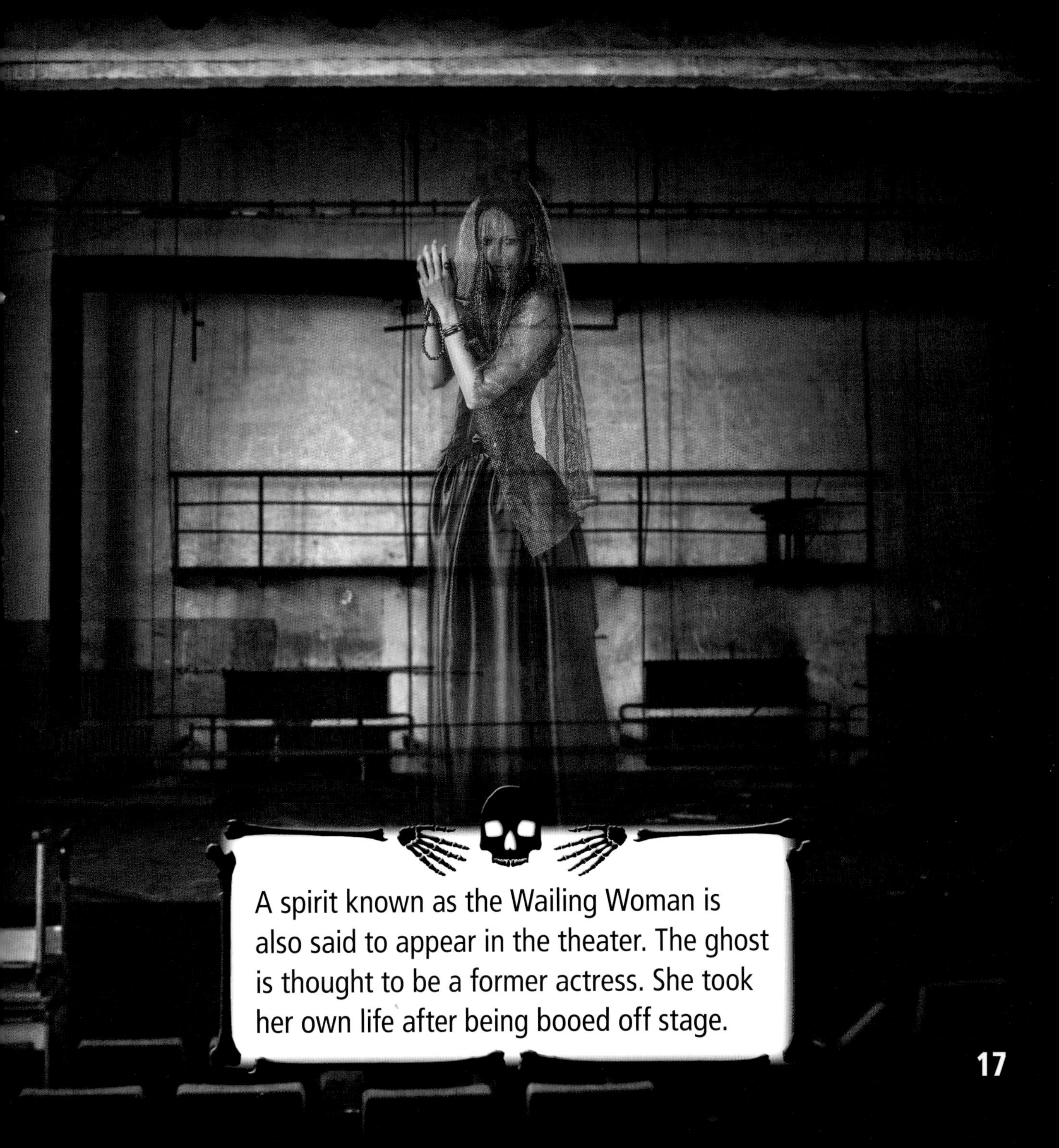

A spirit known as the Wailing Woman is also said to appear in the theater. The ghost is thought to be a former actress. She took her own life after being booed off stage.

Dead But Not Gone

KiMo Theatre, Albuquerque, New Mexico

One day in 1951, a six-year-old boy named Bobby Darnell went to see a movie at the KiMo Theatre. He was in the **lobby** when there was a loud boom. An explosion ripped through the theater! Bobby's lifeless body was found in the **debris.**

The KiMo Theatre

Inside the KiMo Theatre

The explosion was caused when the theater's **boiler** blew up.

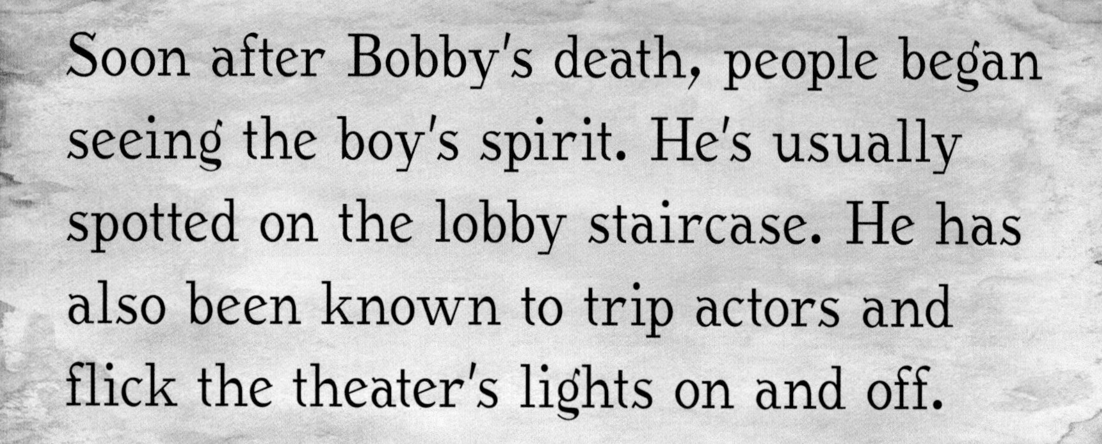

Soon after Bobby's death, people began seeing the boy's spirit. He's usually spotted on the lobby staircase. He has also been known to trip actors and flick the theater's lights on and off.

The staircase in the theater's lobby

People began leaving treats for the child ghost. Sometimes, they even strung up doughnuts for him behind the stage. The next day, the doughnuts were either gone . . . or had child-size bites in them.

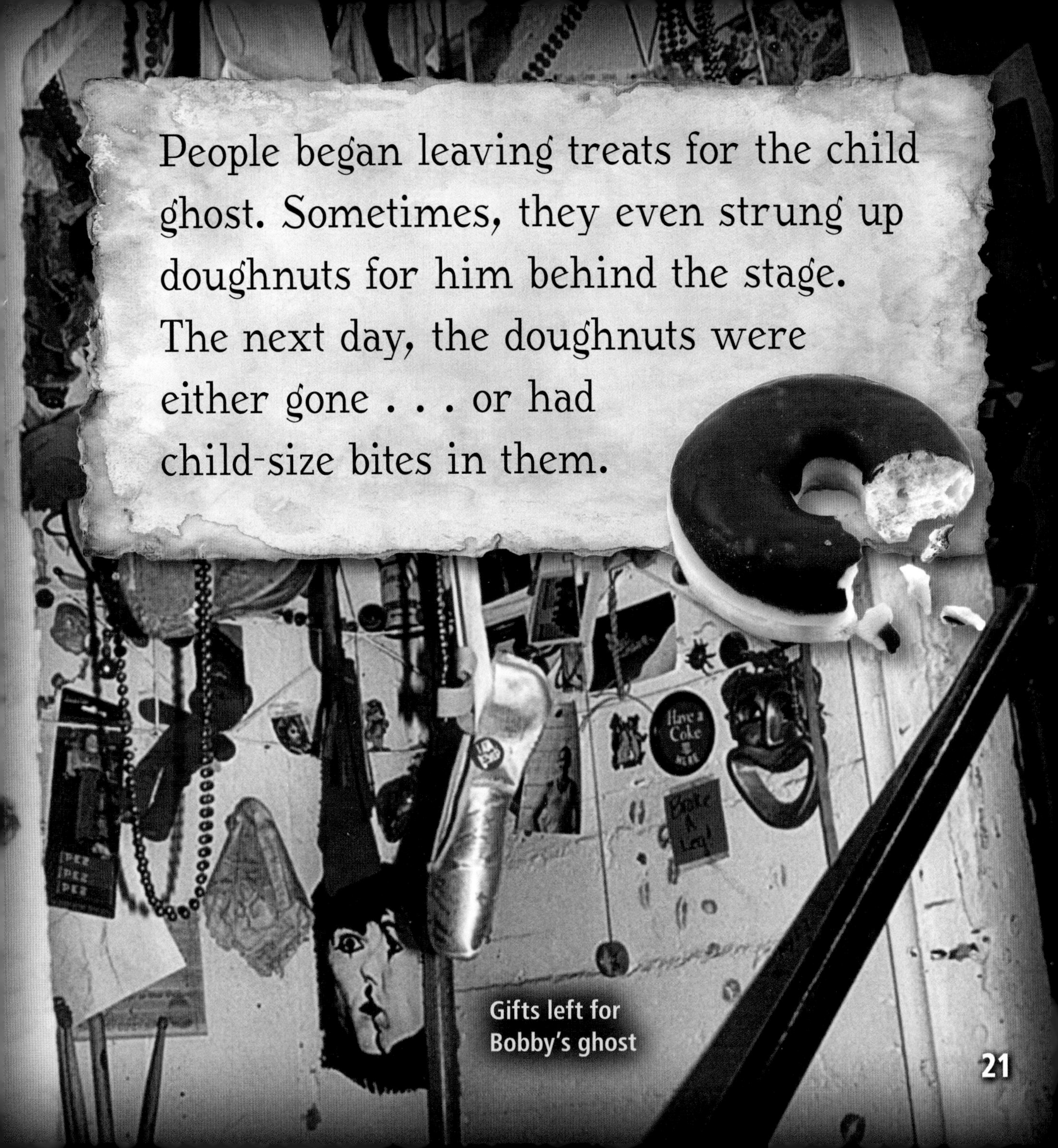

Gifts left for Bobby's ghost

Ghostly Theaters Around the World

KiMo Theatre
Albuquerque, New Mexico

Visit a theater where a ghostly child plays tricks.

New Amsterdam Theatre
New York, New York

Check out a stage where a showgirl's spirit lingers!

Ford's Theatre
Washington, DC

Watch President Lincoln's ghostly assassination play out.

St. James Theatre
Wellington, New Zealand

Explore one of New Zealand's most haunted theaters.

Glossary

assassination (uh-sass-uh-NAY-shuhn) the act of murder

boiler (BOI-lur) a machine that uses steam to heat a building

Civil War (SIV-il WOR) the U.S. war between the northern states and the southern states, which lasted from 1861 to 1865

debris (duh-BREE) broken pieces of something

eerily (EAR-uh-lee) frighteningly

grasped (GRASPD) held

lobby (LOB-ee) a large room at the front of a building where people gather

lurking (LURK-ing) secretly hiding

spirit (SPIHR-it) a supernatural being such as a ghost

tragic (TRAJ-ik) very sad or unfortunate

Index

Read More

Lunis, Natalie. *Tragic Theaters (Scary Places).* New York: Bearport (2014).

Teitelbaum, Michael. *The Secret of the Tragic Theater (Cold Whispers).* New York: Bearport (2016).

Learn More Online

To learn more about ghostly theaters, visit:
www.bearportpublishing.com/Tiptoe

About the Author

Kathryn Camisa once stayed at a castle believed to be haunted. Unfortunately, she did not meet any ghosts during her visit.